Pebble® Plus

Creepy Crawlers

Tarantulas

by Jeni Wittrock

Gail Saunders-Smith, PhD, Consulting Editor

Consultant: Wade Harrell
Vice President
American Tarantula Society

CAPSTONE PRESS
a capstone imprint

Pebble Plus is published by Capstone Press,
1710 Roe Crest Drive, North Mankato, Minnesota 56003.
www.capstonepub.com

Library of Congress Cataloging-in-Publication Data
Wittrock, Jeni.
Tarantulas / by Jeni Wittrock.
p. cm.—(Pebble plus. Creepy crawlers)
Summary: "Learn about tarantulas, including how and where they live and how these creepy creatures are important parts of their world"—Provided by publisher.
Audience: 005-008.
Audience: K to grade 3.
Includes bibliographical references and index.
ISBN 978-1-4765-2458-0 (library binding)
ISBN 978-1-4765-3495-4 (eBook PDF)
1. Tarantulas—Juvenile literature. I. Title.
QL458.42.T5W58 2014
595.4'4—dc23   2013005523

Editorial Credits
Jeni Wittrock, editor; Kyle Grenz, designer; Laura Manthe, production specialist

Photo Credits
Capstone Studio: Karon Dubke, 1, cover; Chad Campbell, 11, 13; Corbis: Michael & Patricia Fogden, 7, Visuals Unlimited/ Robert Pickett, 21; Science Source: Francesco Tomasinelli, 9, 19; Shutterstock: Amir Ridhwan, 5, formiktopus, 15, Ryan M. Bolton, 17, vlastas66, design element (throughout)

This book was written in memory of the author's first pet tarantula, Santiago—a gentle male *Grammostola rosea* who proved that fears can be overcome.

Note to Parents and Teachers

The Creepy Crawlers set supports national science standards related to life science. This book describes and illustrates tarantulas. The images support early readers in understanding the text. The repetition of words and phrases helps early readers learn new words. This book also introduces early readers to subject-specific vocabulary words, which are defined in the Glossary section. Early readers may need assistance to read some words and to use the Table of Contents, Glossary, Read More, Internet Sites, and Index sections of the book.

Printed in China by Nordica.
0413/CA21300494
032013   007226NORDF13

Table of Contents

Hairy and Scary 4

Tarantula Homes 6

Body Parts 10

Dinner Time .14

Eggs to Adults 18

Glossary 22

Read More 23

Internet Sites 23

Index 24

Hairy and Scary

What has eight fuzzy legs, eight beady eyes, and two sharp fangs? It is a tarantula, the biggest and hairiest of all spiders.

Tarantula Homes

Tarantulas live in warm, wet, or dry climates. These arachnids are found in North and South America, Africa, Asia, and Australia.

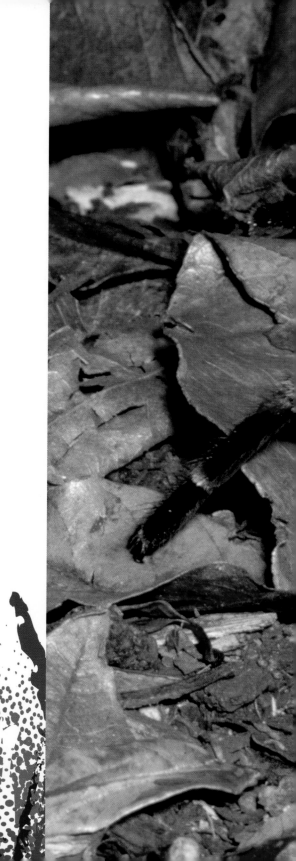

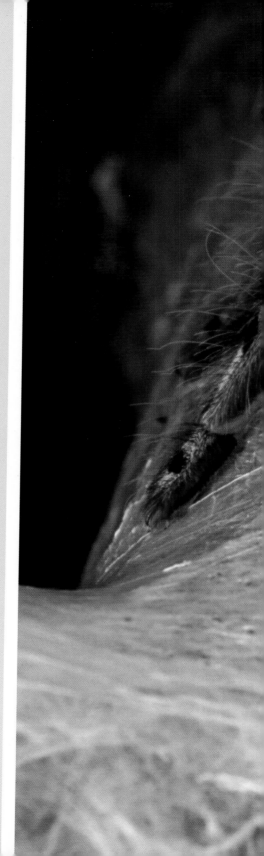

Tarantulas live deep in burrows,
high in trees, or on the ground.
There are more than 900 kinds
of tarantulas. More are discovered
every year.

9

Body Parts

Tarantula bodies have two sections.

The prosoma is the front part.

It holds a tarantula's eyes, fangs,

mouth, legs, and pedipalps.

Pedipalps look like short legs.

leg

eight eyes

prosoma

pedipalps

11

The other half of a tarantula's body is the abdomen. It has spinnerets for making silk. Underneath, there are organs called book lungs for breathing.

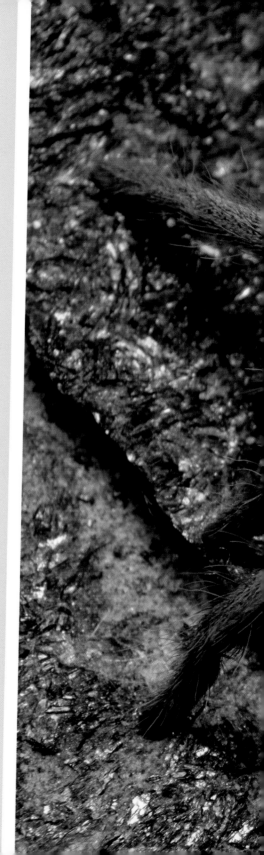

the underside of a tarantula

mouth

book lungs

fangs

spinnerets

abdomen

13

Dinner Time

Tarantulas are insect hunters. But they don't spot prey with their eyes. Hairs called setae feel prey moving. Setae tell tarantulas where to strike.

say it like this
setae — SEE-tay

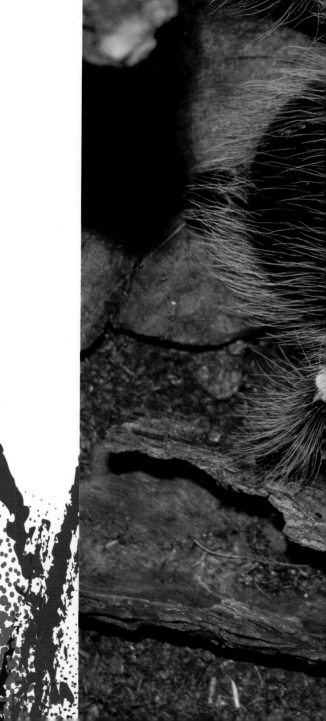

setae

Bam! Tarantulas use their legs to grab bugs. Their fangs bite deep. Venom in the fangs makes prey unable to move. The spiders suck out the bug's juicy insides. Slurp!

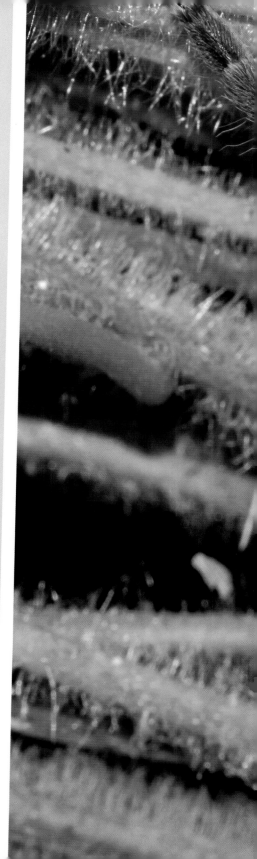

Eggs to Adults

A female tarantula lays from 50 to 2,000 eggs. She keeps the eggs in a sac made of silk. She carries the sac until the eggs hatch.

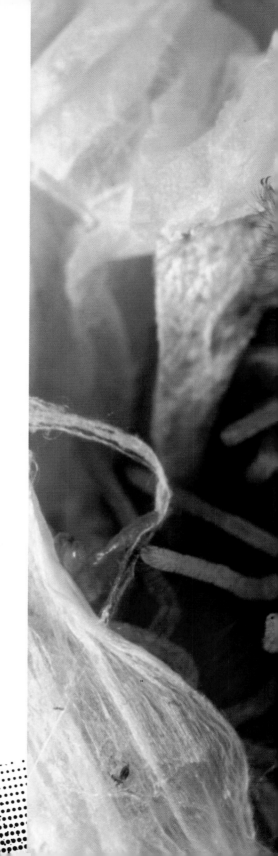

baby tarantulas in an egg sac

Tarantula spiderlings take care
of themselves. Males usually live
for 5 to 15 years. Females can
live for 20 years or more.
Tarantulas are creepy but cool!

a tarantula spiderling

21

Glossary

abdomen—the lower half of a tarantula's body

arachnid—a group of animals that includes spiders, scorpions, mites, and ticks

climate—the average weather of a place throughout the year

fang—a clawlike tooth that squirts out venom

insect—a small animal with a hard outer shell, six legs, three body sections, and two antennae

pedipalp—a short, leglike limb that helps tarantulas hold their prey and mate

prey—an animal hunted by another animal for food

prosoma—the upper half of a tarantula's body

sac—a pouch made of silk that holds spider eggs

seta—one of many hairs that feel movement and vibrations, or setae

silk—a thin but strong thread made by spiders

spiderling—a young tarantula

spinneret—one of two stubby organs that squirt out silk

strike—to attack

venom—a liquid poison made by an animal to kill its prey

Read More

Britton, Tamara L. *Bird-eating Spiders.* Spiders, Set 1. Edina, Minn.: ABDO Pub., 2011.

Camisa, Kathryn. *Hairy Tarantulas.* No Backbone! New York: Bearport Pub., 2009.

Hewitt, Sally. *Bugs Pop-Up: Creepy Crawlers Face to Face.* Harry N. Abrams: New York, 2010.

Internet Sites

FactHound offers a safe, fun way to find Internet sites related to this book. All of the sites on FactHound have been researched by our staff.

Here's all you do:

Visit *www.facthound.com*

Type in this code: 9781476524580

Index

abdomens, 12

arachnids, 6

book lungs, 12

burrows, 8

egg sacs, 18

eyes, 4, 10, 14

fangs, 4, 10, 16

females, 18, 20

hatching, 18

homes, 6, 8

hunting, 14, 16

kinds of tarantulas, 8

legs, 4, 10, 16

lifespans, 20

males, 20

mouths, 10

pedipalps, 10

prey, 14, 16

prosomas, 10

setae, 14

silk, 12, 18

spiderlings, 20

spinnerets, 12

venom, 16

Word Count: 229
Grade: 1
Early-Intervention Level: 19